PSALMS

DEEPENING LIFE TOGETHER

PSALMS

LifeTogether

a division of Baker Publishing Group
Grand Rapids, Michigan

Published by Baker Books
a division of Baker Publishing Group
P.O. Box 6287, Grand Rapids, MI 49516-6287
www.bakerbooks.com

Printed in the United States of America

Library of Congress Cataloging-in-Publication Data

Psalms.
     p.   cm. — (Deepening life together)
    Includes bibliographical references.
    ISBN 978-0-8010-6855-3 (pbk.)
    1. Bible. O.T. Psalms—Textbooks.
    BS1451.P74 2011
    223′.20071—dc22
                                           2011006278

11 12 13 14 15 16 17   7 6 5 4 3 2 1

CONTENTS

ACKNOWLEDGMENTS

The *Deepening Life Together: Psalms* Small Group Video Bible Study has come together through the efforts of many at Baker Publishing Group, Lifetogether Publishing, and Lamplighter Media for which we express our heartfelt thanks.

Executive Producer	John Nill
Producer and Director	Sue Doc Ross
Editors	Mark L. Strauss (Scholar), Teresa Haymaker
Curriculum Development	Brett Eastman, Sue Doc Ross, Mark L. Strauss, Teresa Haymaker, Stephanie French, Karen Lee-Thorp
Video Production	Chris Balish, Rodney Bissell, Nick Calabrese, Sebastian Hoppe Fuentes, Josh Greene, Patrick Griffin, Teresa Haymaker, Oziel Jabin Ibarra, Natali Ibarra, Janae Janik, Keith Sorrell, Lance Tracy, Sophie Olson, Ian Ross
Teachers and Scholars	Mark L. Strauss, David Talley, Tremper Longman III, Daniel Watson, Joanne Jung, Kenneth Way, Craig Keener, Richard Rigsby
Baker Publishing Group	Jack Kuhatschek

Special thanks to: DeLisa Ivy, Bethel Seminary, Talbot School of Theology, Wheaton College

Clips from The JESUS Film are copyright © 1995–2010 The JESUS Film Project®. A ministry of Campus Crusade for Christ International®.

Interior icons by Tom Clark

READ ME FIRST

Welcome to the *Deepening Life Together* study on *Psalms*. For some of you, this might be the first time you've connected in a small group community. We want you to know that God cares about you and your spiritual growth. As you prayerfully respond to the principles you learn in this study, God will move you to a deeper level of commitment and intimacy with himself, as well as with those in your small group.

We at Baker Books and Lifetogether Publishing look forward to hearing the stories of how God changes you from the inside out during this small group experience. We pray God blesses you with all he has planned for you through this journey together.

> For the LORD is good and his love endures forever;
> his faithfulness continues through all generations.
>
> Psalm 100:5

Session Outline

Most people want to live a healthy, balanced spiritual life, but few achieve this by themselves. And most small groups struggle to balance all of God's purposes in their meetings. Groups tend to overemphasize one of the five purposes, perhaps fellowship or discipleship.

Rarely is there a healthy balance that includes evangelism, ministry, and worship. That's why we've included all of these elements in this study so you can live a healthy, balanced spiritual life over time.

A typical group session will include the following:

Memory Verses

For each session we have provided a Memory Verse that emphasizes an important truth from the session. This is an optional exercise, but we believe that memorizing Scripture can be a vital part of filling our minds with God's Word. We encourage you to give this important habit a try.

 ## CONNECTING *with God's Family (Fellowship)*

The foundation for spiritual growth is an intimate connection with God and his family. A few people who really know you and who earn your trust provide a place to experience the life Jesus invites you to live. This section of each session typically offers you two activities.

You can get to know your whole group by using the icebreaker question, and/or you can check in with one or two group members—your spiritual partner(s)—for a deeper connection and encouragement in your spiritual journey.

DVD Teaching Segment

A *Deepening Life Together: Psalms* Video Teaching DVD companion to this study guide is available. For each study session, the DVD contains a lesson taught by Mark Strauss. If you are using the DVD, you will view the teaching segment after your *Connecting* discussion and before your group discussion time (the *Growing* section).

 ## GROWING *to Be Like Christ (Discipleship)*

Here is where you come face-to-face with Scripture. In core passages you'll explore what the Bible teaches about the topic of the study.

The focus won't be on accumulating information but on how we should live in light of the Word of God. We want to help you apply the Scriptures practically, creatively, and from your heart as well as your head. At the end of the day, allowing the timeless truths from God's Word to transform our lives in Christ is our greatest aim.

DEVELOPING *Your Gifts to Serve Others (Ministry)*

Jesus trained his disciples to discover and develop their gifts to serve others. And God has designed each of us uniquely to serve him in a way no other person can. This section will help you discover and use your God-given design. It will also encourage your group to discover your unique design as a community. In this study, you'll put into practice what you've learned in the Bible study by taking a step to serve others. These simple steps will take your group on a faith journey that could change your lives forever.

SHARING *Your Life Mission Every Day (Evangelism)*

Many people skip over this aspect of the Christian life because it's scary, relationally awkward, or simply too much work for their busy schedules. But Jesus wanted all of his disciples to help outsiders connect with him, to know him personally. This doesn't mean preaching on street corners. It could mean welcoming a few newcomers into your group, hosting a short-term group in your home, or walking through this study with a friend. In this study, you'll have an opportunity to go beyond Bible study to biblical living.

SURRENDERING *Your Life for God's Pleasure (Worship)*

God is most pleased by a heart that is fully his. Each group session will give you a chance to surrender your heart to God in prayer and worship. You may read a psalm together, share a page in your journal, or sing a song to close your meeting. If you have never prayed aloud in a group before, no one will pressure you. Instead, you'll experience the support of others who are praying for you.

Study Notes

This section provides background notes on the Bible passage(s) you examine in the *Growing* section. You may want to refer to these notes during your group meeting or as a reference for those doing additional study.

For Deeper Study (optional)

Some sessions provide *For Deeper Study*. If you want to dig deeper into more Bible passages about the topic at hand, we've provided additional passages and questions. Your group may choose to do study homework ahead of each meeting in order to cover more biblical material. Or you as an individual may choose to study the *For Deeper Study* on your own. If you prefer not to do study homework, the *Growing* section will provide you with plenty to discuss within the group. These options allow individuals or the whole group to go deeper in their study, while still accommodating those who can't do homework or are new to your group. You can record your discoveries in your journal. We encourage you to read some of your insights to a friend (spiritual partner) for accountability and support. Spiritual partners may check in each week over the phone, through e-mail, or at the beginning of the group meeting.

Reflections

On the *Reflections* pages we provide Scriptures to read and reflect on between group meetings. We suggest you use this section to seek God at home throughout the week. This time at home should begin and end with prayer. Don't get in a hurry; take enough time to hear God's direction.

Subgroup for Discussion and Prayer

If your group is large (more than seven people), we encourage you to separate into groups of two to four for discussion and prayer. This is to encourage greater participation and deeper discussion.

INTRODUCTION

Jesus's disciples asked, "Lord, teach us to pray" (Luke 11:1). Prayer is simply talking to God, and worship is simply bowing down before God's majesty, so we might think we don't need to be taught how to do these things, but we'd be wrong. Many of us feel inarticulate standing before God and trying to put our heart's cry into words. The Psalms teach us a vocabulary of prayer and worship that we can use both in private and corporately.

The Psalms were composed by various authors for a variety of purposes for both public and private life in ancient Israel. There are several kinds of psalms, and scholars use several designations for different types. Some psalms combine characteristics from more than one type.

In this study we'll look at four types: *Psalms of Praise* (session 1), *Psalms of Lament* (session 2), *Psalms of Thanksgiving* (session 3), and *Royal Psalms* (session 4).

Psalms of praise (sometimes called hymns) celebrate who God is and his provision for life. They are often called songs of orientation because they point us toward God.

The most common psalms are laments, cries to God for help. We sing lament psalms when life is difficult and disappointing. Many include desperate appeals, like "How long, Lord?" and "Why, Lord?" while others contain angry cries to God to punish the wicked that are persecuting the psalmist. These types of psalms are referred to as songs of disorientation.

Psalms of thanksgiving are expressions of joy sung in response to God's answer to our laments. As he faithfully provides and answers our laments, he "reorients" the psalmist's life. Thus, these are songs of reorientation.

Psalms that celebrate the human king's role in God's rule over his people are called royal psalms. These royal psalms often point beyond the king who was alive when they were written toward the hope for the Messiah. The Messiah or "Anointed One" is God's final regent who will reign on David's throne with justice and righteousness forever.

There are also some types that we won't cover in this study. For example, wisdom psalms are directed, not to God, but to other human beings to contrast godly living and the fate of the wicked. In psalms of remembrance, the singer looks at God's great acts in history (such as the exodus from Egypt) and, through reflection on the past, gains confidence for the present and hope for the future.

As we learn the purposes and heart behind these psalms, we can come away with a new, colorful, and expressive vocabulary through which we will be able to boldly approach God no matter what we face.

PSALMS OF PRAISE

MEMORY VERSE: Let everything that has breath praise the LORD (Ps. 150:6).

The song "Happy Birthday to You," which is sung in celebration of loved ones hundreds of millions of times each year, is unarguably the most recognized song in the English language, and quite possibly in the world. Second to this is the song, "For He's a Jolly Good Fellow," which honors the achievements of our colleagues and friends. These are considered songs of praise—words of adoration or celebration for someone's accomplishments or milestones in life.

Celebration through song is a very natural thing for people. When we observe national holidays or honor servicemen and women, we sing songs that commemorate our nation's heritage. At the passage of a new year, we sing in remembrance of where we've been, what we've done, and in anticipation of what is to come.

In today's session, we will look at psalms that celebrate God—or psalms of praise that celebrate who God is and his provision for life. They are often called songs of orientation because they point us toward God.

CONNECTING

10 min.

Open your group with prayer, asking God to put his finger on the areas of your life that he might want to transform through the study of the *Psalms of Praise*.

As you begin, take time to pass around a sheet of paper on which to write down your contact information, including the best time and method for contacting you. Or pass around one of your study guides opened to the *Small Group Roster*. Then, someone volunteer to make copies or type up a list with everyone's information and e-mail it to the group this week.

1. Begin this first session by introducing yourselves. Include your name, what you do for a living, and what you do for fun. You may also include whether or not you are married, how long you have been married, how many children you have, and their ages. Also share what brought you to this *Deepening Life Together: Psalms* small group study and what you expect to learn during the next few weeks.

2. Share a time when you celebrated some person or situation through spoken words of praise or song. How did you feel?

3. Whether your group is new or ongoing, it's always important to reflect on and review your values together. In the *Appendix* is a *Small Group Agreement* with the values we've found most useful in sustaining healthy, balanced groups. We recommend that you review these values and choose one or two—values you haven't previously focused on or have room to grow in—to emphasize during this study. Choose values that will take your group to the next stage of intimacy and spiritual health.

GROWING

45–50 min.

Praise is genuine expression of celebration for who God is and what he does. It's how we communicate our joy and gratitude to God for his goodness, faithfulness, and righteousness. Psalms of praise, or hymns, celebrate God through words of adoration. Most, if not all, of the psalms were originally written as lyrics set to music. Many praise psalms even mention singing and the playing of instruments such as the harp and trumpet. In this session we'll look closely at two praise psalms to see what elements they contain and how they can train us to praise God more deeply.

Read Psalm 8 aloud.

4. Psalm 8 praises God for his grace in placing humanity in a position of authority over God's great creation. What words or phrases does the psalmist use that indicate this is a psalm of praise?

   In what specific ways does this psalm celebrate God?

5. Psalm 8:1 says: "You have set your glory above the heavens." Considering this, why can we offer praise to God over and over again and never exhaust ourselves?

6. The psalmist was brought to praise as he considered the lowliness of humanity. Why do you think that is?

   Why is awe before God such an important attitude for us to cultivate?

7. Psalm 8:6 tells us that the works of God's hands have been placed under humanity's authority. What does this mean?

   What responsibilities go along with this authority?

8. Psalm 8:3 provides imagery that gives us insight into the psalmist's activities when he wrote it. What was the author doing?

   What activities will foster your own spirit of praise to God for your position of authority over the many wonders of God's creation?

Read Psalm 46 aloud.

9. Psalm 46 is a confession of fearless trust in a mighty God during a time of upheaval. Two specific types of help are mentioned in verse 1. What are they? Describe them in your own words.

10. Psalm 46:4 says: "There is a river whose streams make glad the city of God." This river is probably a metaphor of the continuous outpouring of God's blessings over the holy city, Jerusalem, during a time when the city was in uproar. How does this verse apply to us today?

11. What does Psalm 46:8–10 say results from God's mighty acts on behalf of his people?

12. Three times in Psalm 46 we find the word "Selah," which is thought to be an intentional pause for the purpose of reflection. (See *Study Notes*.) How can intentionally placed pauses in our lives help us to remember God as our fortress in times of trouble and our source of strength to endure them?

13. Praise psalms can be called psalms of orientation, because they orient us to what is really true and important. How do Psalms 18 and 46 do this?

DEVELOPING

10 min.

Accountability means being answerable to another for our actions. Spiritual accountability happens when we invite someone into our life for the purpose of encouraging our faith journey and challenging us in specific areas of desired growth. Hebrews 3:12–13 says: "See to it, brothers, that none of you has a sinful, unbelieving heart that turns away from the living God. But encourage one another daily, as long as it is called Today, so that none of you may be hardened by sin's deceitfulness." Opening our lives to someone and making ourselves vulnerable to their loving admonition could perhaps be one of the most difficult things to do; however, it could also result in the deepest and most lasting spiritual growth we've known.

14. Scripture tells us in Ephesians 4:25: "Laying aside falsehood, speak truth each one of you with his neighbor, for we are members of one another" (NASB). One important way to discover and develop our God-given design is to partner with another Christian for spiritual connection and accountability. We call this a spiritual partnership. We strongly recommend each of you partner with someone in the group to help you in your spiritual journey during this study. This person will be your spiritual partner for the next several weeks. He or she doesn't have to be your best friend but will simply encourage you to complete the goals you set for yourself during this study. Following through on a resolution is tough when you're on your own, but we've found it makes all the difference to have a partner cheering us on. See the *Leader's Notes* for instructions for establishing spiritual partners.

15. In the *Appendix* we've provided a *Personal Health Plan*, a chart for keeping track of your spiritual progress. You and your spiritual partner can use it for accountability to the goals you set for yourselves. See the *Personal Health Plan* for instructions. If time permits, complete the "Connect" and "Grow" questions of your *Personal Health Plan* and share your answers with your spiritual partner.

SHARING   10 *min.*

Each of us have people in our lives that don't know Christ. These people make up your circles of influence or *Circles of Life*. Jesus wants all of us to be instruments in bringing them closer to a relationship with him.

16. Use the *Circles of Life* diagram on the following page to help you think of people you come in contact with on a regular basis who need to be connected in Christian community. Try to write two names in each circle. Consider the following ideas for reaching out to one or two of the people you list and make a plan to follow through with them this week.

Family
(immediate or extended)
_____
_____
_____

Acquaintances
(neighbors, kids' sports
teams, school, and so forth)
_____
_____
_____

Friends
_____
_____
_____

Fun
(gym, hobbies, hangouts)
_____
_____
_____

Co-workers
(workplace)
_____
_____
_____

☐ This is a wonderful time to welcome a few friends into your group. Which of the people on your list could you invite? It's possible that you may need to help your friend overcome obstacles to come to a place where he or she can encounter Jesus. Does your friend need a ride to the group or help with child care?

☐ Consider inviting a friend to attend a weekend church service with you and possibly plan to enjoy a meal together afterward. This can be a great opportunity to talk with someone about your faith in Jesus.

☐ Is there someone who is unable to attend your group but who still needs a connection? Would you be willing to have lunch or coffee with that person, catch up on life, and share something you've learned from this study? Jesus doesn't call

all of us to lead small groups, but he does call every disciple to spiritually multiply his or her life over time.

SURRENDERING

10 min.

Deuteronomy 32:3–4 declares: "I will proclaim the name of the LORD. Oh, praise the greatness of our God! He is the Rock, his works are perfect, and all his ways are just." Only our perfect God is worthy of praise.

17. Focus on the words of David as you read Psalm 145 aloud together in an attitude of praise and worship.

18. Every believer should have a plan for spending time alone with God. At the end of each session we have provided *Reflections* for you to begin daily time with him. There are five daily Scripture readings with room to record your thoughts. These will offer reinforcement of the principles we are learning and develop the habit of time alone with God throughout the week.

19. Answer this question: "How can we pray for you this week?" Write prayer requests on your *Prayer and Praise Report* and commit to praying for each other throughout the week. Close with a prayer of praise to God.

Study Notes

Selah: (sē´-luh) This word is only found in the poetical books of the Old Testament. It is probably a musical notation indicating an intended pause, or interlude—a pause in the voices singing, while the instruments perform alone—though the meaning is a matter of conjecture, as there is no way to know for sure.

For Deeper Study (Optional)

Read and reflect on how each of the following psalms expresses praise to God.

- Psalm 146: God the Helper
- Psalm 147: God the Almighty
- Psalm 148: God the Creator
- Psalm 149: God the Victorious
- Psalm 150: Everyone praise God!

Reflections

Reading, reflecting, and meditating on the Word of God is essential to getting to know him deeply. As you read the verses each day, give prayerful consideration to what you learn about God, his Spirit, and his place in your life. Then record your thoughts, insights, or prayer in the *Reflect* section below the verses you read. On the sixth day, record a summary of what you learned over the entire week through this study.

Day 1. The heavens declare the glory of God; the skies proclaim the work of his hands (Ps. 19:1).

REFLECT

_____

_____

_____

_____

Day 2. Shout for joy to the LORD, all the earth, burst into jubilant song with music (Ps. 98:4).

REFLECT

_____

_____

_____

_____

Day 3. Praise the LORD. Praise the LORD, O my soul. I will praise the LORD all my life; I will sing praise to my God as long as I live (Ps. 146:1–2).

REFLECT

_____

_____

_____

_____

Day 4. Praise the LORD. How good it is to sing praises to our God, how pleasant and fitting to praise him! (Ps. 147:1)

REFLECT

_____

_____

_____

_____

Day 5. Let everything that has breath praise the LORD. Praise the LORD (Ps. 150:6).

REFLECT

_____

_____

_____

_____

Day 6. Use the following space to write any thoughts God has put in your heart and mind about the things we have looked at in this session and during your *Reflections* time this week.

SUMMARY

_____

_____

_____

_____

PSALMS OF LAMENT

MEMORY VERSE: Because of the LORD's great love we are not consumed, for his compassions never fail. They are new every morning (Lam. 3:22–23).

A husband and father walks through the front door early with news that he has lost his job and ability to provide for his family. In what seems like a moment, a wife loses her husband to a massive heart attack. In the doctor's office, parents receive news that their child is critically ill. In the hours following a fatal car crash, a teenager reflects on his poor choice to drink and drive. None of us is a stranger to pain and suffering. We ask, "Why, Lord?" "How long must I endure this pain?" Where do we turn when our hearts are so heavy, so full of pain, that we cannot even find the words to express ourselves?

God knows our pain and suffering. He understands the weight of our pain and has given us a vent to our suffering through the psalms of lament. Often in the book of Psalms we see our own words, our own feelings, of despair and loneliness reflected back to us when we can't find our own words, or are perhaps just afraid to validate them by saying them aloud. Laments represent honest communication with God during life's most difficult situations.

CONNECTING

Begin your group meeting in prayer. Ask God to open your hearts and minds to the message he has for us this week.

1. Describe a time when a psalm reflected or illuminated your feelings in a painful situation.

2. Sit with your spiritual partner. If your partner is absent or if you are new to the group, join with another pair or someone who doesn't yet have a partner. (If you haven't established your spiritual partnerships yet, turn to the *Session One Leader's Notes* in the *Appendix* for information on how to begin your partnerships.)

    Turn to your *Personal Health Plan* in the *Appendix*. Share with your partner how your time with God went this week. What is one thing you discovered? Did you make a commitment to a next step that you can share? Make a note about your partner's progress and how you can pray for him or her.

GROWING

The most common psalms in the Psalter are "laments," in which God's people cry out to him for help in their pain and suffering. They sometimes question God's wisdom and challenge him to act on the psalmist's behalf. Though the psalmists cry to God for help, they don't despair. Instead, they include a confident statement of hope that God will intervene. While praise psalms are about orientation to what is true and real, laments express the honest disorientation we feel when life gets painful and confusing.

Read Psalm 3 aloud.

3. What is the psalmist's obvious need in verses 1–2?

    The psalmist likely faced his enemies in an imminent military battle. What enemies do we face in our lives today?

4. What statement of confident hope does the psalmist make in verses 3–4?

How does this confidence encourage you as you face the enemies that surround you?

5. Verse 5 is another statement that communicates confident hope in God. How does this example of confidence apply to you?

How do you think a person develops this depth of confidence in God amid dangers?

6. Note that the psalmist does not ask God for immunity from danger. What is his petition in verses 7–8?

7. In Psalm 3 the psalmist directs us to pause for reflection several times (see the *Study Notes* for *Session One*). Why do you think it is important that we take intentional breaks to reflect during our times of distress or suffering?

Read Psalm 88 aloud.

8. Psalm 88 is the saddest of the Psalms. It expresses the darkest anguish of a believer who feels abandoned by God. What emotions is the psalmist feeling, and how does he convey them?

9. What can we learn about God from the fact that he welcomes this kind of candid expression of pain and questioning?

10. Despite the pain in this candid psalm, the slightest glimmer of hope can be found if we pay close attention. What does the psalmist say that gives us insight into the seeds of hope in the deepest recesses of his heart?

11. Who is responsible for the psalmist's troubled life, according to verses 6–9a? Why do you think he believes this?

12. Most psalmists resolve their complaints by moving toward a maturity of faith or confident hope, but this one does not. It

is the only psalm in which the psalmist remains in a state of despair from the first line to the last. What special lesson can we learn from the inclusion of this psalm in Scripture?

SHARING   *10 min.*

All believers are Christ's messengers or ambassadors to the world. We are not responsible for the acceptance of the message we share, but we are to be obedient in sharing it. One thing we can learn from Scripture is: Never give up on sharing Jesus with others, even when it seems that no one is listening.

13. God raised Jesus from the dead, and Jesus appeared to the apostles and those who had travelled with him (Acts 13:31). They became eyewitnesses that Jesus really was raised from the dead as Savior and Lord. In what sense can we be witnesses of Jesus today?

    To what group of people or area of mission has God called you? If you have no idea, how could you begin to find out?

14. Return to the *Circles of Life* and review the names of those you chose to invite to this group, to church, or for one-on-one discipleship. How did it go? Share how your invitations went. If you are attending this group for the first time because someone invited you, feel free to share your perspective on this question.
    If you haven't followed through, think about what is preventing you from doing so. As a group, consider some ways to overcome obstacles or excuses that keep us from reaching out and inviting people into our Christian community.

15. The apostle Paul's message throughout his ministry was always that through Jesus we have forgiveness of sins (Acts 13:38–39). Through him, everyone who believes is made right with God. Have you received God's forgiveness and justification through Christ Jesus? How can you be sure?

DEVELOPING

10 min.

God created each of us to serve him within the body of Christ. It is because of the vast number of needs represented by the countless people and circumstances around us that God has given every believer unique gifts. Each of us has something very special to offer to fill specific needs within the church.

16. Is there an area of service that God has put on your heart to serve this group or your local church? Commit to taking the first step, and be willing to let God lead you to the ministry that expresses your passion. In your *Personal Health Plan* next to the "Develop" icon, answer the WHERE question: "WHERE are you serving?" If you are not currently serving, note one area where you will consider serving.

SURRENDERING

10 min.

James 5:16 says, "Confess your sins to each other and pray for each other so that you may be healed. The prayer of a righteous man is powerful and effective."

17. No doubt there are members of your group who are struggling with life situations right now. Take some time to pray for one another. Allow each person or couple the opportunity to share any pressing needs, concerns, or struggles requiring prayer, and the rest of the group can pray for these requests. Don't forget to write down the requests so that group members can be praying throughout the week.

Study Notes

Psalter: A book containing the book of Psalms or a particular version of, musical setting for, or selection from it.

For Deeper Study (Optional)

Read and reflect on the lament in Psalm 77, a psalm that looks to God's great acts (particularly the Exodus) to gain confidence in the present and hope for the future.

- Crying out to God with uplifted hands, vv. 1–6
- Accusing God of letting him down, vv. 7–9
- Remembering God's great acts in the past (the Exodus), vv. 10–12, 16–20
- God is great, vv. 13–15

Reflections

Hopefully last week you made a commitment to read, reflect, and meditate on the Word of God each day. Following are selections of Scripture provided as a starting point to drawing near to God through time with him. Read the daily verses and then record your thoughts, insights, or prayers in the space provided. On the sixth day, record a summary of what you have learned over the entire week through this study or use this space to write down how God has challenged you personally.

Day 1. To the LORD I cry aloud, and he answers me from his holy hill (Ps. 3:4).

REFLECT

_____

_____

_____

_____

Day 2. I am a stranger to my brothers, an alien to my own mother's sons; for zeal for your house consumes me, and the insults of those who insult you fall on me (Ps. 69:8–9).

REFLECT

_____

_____

_____

_____

Day 3. I will remember the deeds of the LORD; yes, I will remember your miracles of long ago (Ps. 77:11).

REFLECT

_____

_____

_____

_____

Day 4. My eyes are dim with grief. I call to you, O LORD, every day; I spread out my hands to you (Ps. 88:9).

REFLECT

_____

_____

_____

_____

Day 5. But I cry to you for help, O LORD; in the morning my prayer comes before you (Ps. 88:13).

REFLECT

_____

_____

_____

_____

Day 6. Use the following space to write any thoughts God has put in your heart and mind about the things we have looked at in this session and during your _Reflections_ time this week.

SUMMARY

_____

_____

_____

_____

PSALMS OF THANKSGIVING

MEMORY VERSE: I will praise God's name in song and glorify him with thanksgiving (Ps. 69:30).

Early one morning, Kristen left her home to drive to her boyfriend's house a few miles away. On the route were a couple of dangerous curves, but Kristen had driven that stretch of road many times before and was confident in her ability to navigate the treacherous road safely. What Kristen didn't realize was that a rainstorm the night before had left the road wet and very slippery. Before she knew it, Kristen's car was hydroplaning and swerving left and right on the two-lane road as she fought to maintain control of her car. The car ran off the road into a very steep ditch and flipped over several times, coming to rest at the base of some trees.

Kristen later recalled, "My whole life flashed before my eyes in a split second. Never before had I been so scared. My car was totaled, but I just ended up with a couple cuts and scrapes on my arms and legs. Many people said it was my seatbelt that saved me, but I know it was by the grace of God that I'm still on this earth and able to see and hug my family and friends. I am so thankful for a second chance at life. I believe God really wanted me to realize that he is always with me."

Kristen's response to her ordeal is a song of thanksgiving to the Lord—an expression of joy sung in response to God's faithfulness to provide and answer our prayers. In this way, God "reorients" our lives after a disorienting event or hardship.

CONNECTING   *10 min.*

Open your group with prayer. Ask God to help you recognize all that you have to be thankful for. Thank God for how he is reshaping your group through this study.

1. When have you experienced a difficult time or hardship in which you later recognized God's love and faithfulness carrying you through?

2. Begin to talk about what's next for your group. Do you want to continue meeting together? If so, the *Small Group Agreement* can help you talk through any changes you might want to make as you move forward. Consider what you will study, who will lead, and where and when you will meet.

GROWING   *45–50 min.*

Psalms of thanksgiving are closely associated with psalms of lament because through them, the psalmist whose lament has been answered offers thanks to God. These psalms can also closely resemble psalms of praise (hymns) because thanks are often offered in the form of lyrical praise. But psalms of thanksgiving are about reorientation—getting things straightened out after a period of disorienting hardship.

Read Psalm 18 aloud.

3. The psalmist uses eight images in verses 1 and 2 to describe who God is for him. What ideas about God do you think these images are meant to give us?

- ☐ strength
- ☐ rock
- ☐ fortress
- ☐ deliverer
- ☐ rock of refuge
- ☐ shield
- ☐ horn (a Hebrew symbol of strength)
- ☐ stronghold

Why is it important to look to God as our source of strength?

4. What are some things other than God that people sometimes look to for strength or safety?

5. The psalmist uses provocative poetry in verses 3–19 to describe God's response to his cry for help. What images do you find most striking?

   Why do you think the author uses such vivid imagery to communicate God's deliverance?

6. What reasons do verses 20–24 give for why God delivers his people?

   Why do you think David is intent on telling the reader these things?

7. Verses 25–31 offer insight into why David explains his deliverance as he does. Do you believe this explanation holds true in every circumstance? Explain your answer.

8. Charles H. Spurgeon once said, "Second thoughts upon God's mercy should be and often are the best."* Psalm 18:32–46 appears to be a retelling of the events of God's deliverance. What

* Charles H. Spurgeon, *Psalms* (Wheaton, IL: Crossway, 1993).

do you notice about this as it compares to the same events depicted in verses 4–19?

How can this type of second look at what God has done in your life offer fresh perspective to your own prayers or psalms of thanksgiving?

9. The psalmist reviews all that God did to enable him to claim victory over his enemies in verses 32–42. Does God enable you in this way to deal with the battles you face?

   If so, how? If not, why do you think he doesn't?

10. Psalm 18:46 says, "The LORD lives!" When have you experienced God in such a way that you were assured that he is alive and active in your life?

   How did it affect your prayers?

If you have time for more study, read Psalm 30 aloud.

11. Psalm 30 is an offering of thankfulness for deliverance from sickness. What evidence do you see in verses 1–3 that indicates the severity of the psalmist's illness?

   Why do you think it is significant that the psalmist uses such severe imagery to depict his plight in a psalm of thanksgiving?

12. What contrasts do you see in this psalm?

13. How does the psalmist portray God's character?

14. According to verses 6–7, the psalmist's time of security made him forget where his security was ultimately found—in the Lord. Then he fell ill and realized the truth. Why do you think God uses difficult circumstances to bring us back into right relationship with him?

15. Verse 12 concludes this psalm with the statement, "my heart may sing to you and *not be silent*" (emphasis added). It's easy to publicly offer prayers of lament, but once our situation has passed, we often forget the hand of God upon our lives and move on without second thought. What has the psalmist's example taught you about the importance of publicly thanking God for your delivery, even if from something minor?

DEVELOPING   *10 min.*

Kingdom-minded people who change the world do so through special gifts God has given us to use as the Holy Spirit leads. The first step in developing the gifts that God has given each of us is to deepen our relationship with him through prayer, reflection, and meditation on his Word.

16. Commit to taking the necessary steps to grow closer to God by beginning one of the following habits this week.

☐ *Prayer.* Commit to personal prayer and daily connection with God. You may find it helpful to write your prayers in a journal.

☐ *Reflection.* Reflections provide an opportunity for reading a short Bible passage five days a week during the course of this study. You also have the opportunity to write down your insights there. On the sixth day you can summarize what God has shown you throughout the week.

☐ *Meditation.* Try meditation as a way of internalizing God's Word more deeply. Copy a portion of Scripture on a card and tape it somewhere in your line of sight, such as your car's dashboard or the kitchen table. Think about it when you sit at red lights, or while you're eating a meal. Reflect on what God is saying to you through his words. Several passages for meditation are suggested on the *Reflections* pages in each session.

17. Check in with your spiritual partner, or with another partner if yours is absent. Talk about any challenges you are currently facing in reaching the goals you set during this study. Tell your spiritual partner how he or she has helped you follow through with each step. Be sure to write down your partner's progress.

SHARING   10 *min.*

Jesus lived and died so that humankind might come to know him and be reconciled to God through him. Through his Holy Spirit, we are empowered to be his witnesses to the people around us.

18. Return to the *Circles of Life* diagram and identify one or two people in each area of your life who need to know Christ. Write their names outside the circles for this exercise. Commit to praying for God's guidance and an opportunity to share with each of them.

19. Inviting people to church or Bible study is one way that we shepherd others toward faith in Christ. On your *Personal Health Plan* next to the "Share" icon, answer the "WHEN are you shepherding another person in Christ?" question.

SURRENDERING   10 *min.*

Philippians 4:6 tells us: "Do not be anxious about anything, but in everything, by prayer and petition, with thanksgiving, present your requests to God." Prayer represents a powerful act of surrender to the Lord as we put aside our pride and lay our burdens at his feet.

20. Share your prayer requests and record them on the *Prayer and Praise Report*. Have any previous prayer requests been answered? If so, celebrate these answers to prayer. Then, in simple, one-sentence prayers, submit your requests to God. Close by thanking God for his commitment to your relationship with him and how he has used this group to teach you more about righteousness.

For Deeper Study (Optional)

Look for some of the characteristics of the psalms we've studied so far in David's song in 2 Samuel 22.

Reflections

If you've been spending time each day connecting with God through his Word, congratulations! Some experts say that it takes twenty-one repetitions to develop a new habit. By the end of this week, you'll be well on your way to cultivating new spiritual habits that will encourage you in your walk with God. This week, continue to read the daily verses, giving prayerful consideration to what you learn about God, his Spirit, and his place in your life. Then, as before, record your thoughts, insights, or prayers in the space provided. On the sixth day, record a summary of what you have learned throughout the week.

Day 1. Give thanks to the LORD, call on his name; make known among the nations what he has done (1 Chron. 16:8).

REFLECT

_____

_____

_____

_____

Day 2. Give thanks to the LORD, for he is good; his love endures forever (Ps. 107:1).

REFLECT

_____

_____

_____

_____

Day 3. Now when Daniel learned that the decree had been published, he went home to his upstairs room where the windows opened toward Jerusalem. Three times a day he got down on his knees and prayed, giving thanks to his God, just as he had done before (Dan. 6:10).

REFLECT

_____

_____

_____

_____

Day 4. Sing and make music in your heart to the Lord, always giving thanks to God the Father for everything, in the name of our Lord Jesus Christ (Eph. 5:19b–20).

REFLECT

_____

_____

_____

Day 5. Be joyful always; pray continually; give thanks in all circumstances, for this is God's will for you in Christ Jesus (1 Thess. 5:16–18).

REFLECT

_____

_____

_____

_____

Day 6. Use the following space to write any thoughts God has put in your heart and mind about the things we have looked at in this session and during your *Reflections* time this week.

SUMMARY

_____

_____

_____

_____

ROYAL PSALMS

MEMORY VERSE: May his name endure forever; may it continue as long as the sun. All nations will be blessed through him, and they will call him blessed (Ps. 72:17).

Psalms that celebrate the human king's role in God's rule over his people are called royal psalms. These royal psalms often point beyond the king who was alive when they were written toward the hope for the Messiah. The Messiah or "Anointed One" is God's final regent who will reign on David's throne with justice and righteousness forever.

This same God who used the kings of old, and ultimately installed our eternal King, Jesus Christ, is just as ready to use any one of us today. Henry Varley once said, "The world has yet to see what God can do with and for and through and in a man who is fully and wholly consecrated to Him." As a young man, D. L. Moody heard Varley's words and aspired to be that man! Moody gave himself entirely over to God's will and the Lord used him mightily. Through God's work in Moody's life fully surrendered, many thousands came to know Jesus Christ as their Savior and King.

CONNECTING   *10 min.*

Open your group with prayer. Thank God for all he has done in your group during this study. Thank him for his Word and the example the psalms provide for your spiritual journey.

1. What present-day leaders do you know who allow God to work through them?

   What kinds of things is God doing in and through them?

2. Take time in this final session to connect with your spiritual partner. Check in with each other about the progress you have made in your spiritual growth during this study. Talk about whether you will continue in your mentoring relationship outside your Bible study group.

GROWING   *45–50 min.*

Throughout history, God, through Christ and the Holy Spirit, has continued to use his people in mighty ways when they open themselves up to his will. In this session we will examine royal psalms that point us toward the Messiah, the great Priest-King, our Savior, Jesus Christ, who would arise from David's line.

Read Psalm 2 aloud.

3. Psalm 2 opens with a rhetorical question: "Why do the nations conspire in vain?" Against whom are the nations rebelling?

   Why is the rebellion in vain?

4. What is God's reaction to the haughty rebellious rulers in verses 4–6?

   What does this tell you about God?

5. In verses 7–9, the Lord's Anointed One speaks. What will be the boundaries of the Anointed One's kingdom?

   How might these verses have applied to the human king alive when the psalm was written?

   How do they seem to speak of things beyond what was true of that king but would someday be true of the Messiah?

6. What warning is issued to the nations' rulers in verses 10–12?

7. To what extent do you think verse 12 could apply to a mortal king, and to what extent does it only make sense about the Messiah?

Read Psalm 45 aloud.

8. The psalm offers words of praise over the bride and groom at a royal wedding. What aspects of the groom's character are praised in verses 2–9?

9. Why do you think it's important that the king's battles were supposed to be won on behalf of truth, humility, and righteousness, and were not supposed to be simply military conquests?

   How does Jesus fulfill this picture of kingship?

10. Verse 6 says, "Your throne, O God, will last for ever and ever." Why do you think the psalmist equated the king's throne with God's throne?

11. What exhortations are given to the bride in verses 10–15?

12. A bride might be hesitant or excited (or both) to "forget her people and her father's house" (v. 10). How do these verses apply to the church today? (See Luke 9:23 and 14:26.)

13. What promises are made through the benediction offered in verses 16–17?

What is your role in perpetuating the memory of the King through all generations?

DEVELOPING   10 *min.*

First Peter 4:10 says: "Each one should use whatever gift he has received to serve others, faithfully administering God's grace in its various forms." We must continually ask ourselves: "Who or where am I serving?" as we go about our daily lives.

14. One way to serve Christ and his flock is through your small group. Meeting and studying God's Word together is important for the discipleship of your group members. Take some time now to consider what's next for your group as this study of Psalms comes to a close. Will you continue to meet together? If so, the *Small Group Agreement* can help you talk through any changes you might want to make as you move forward. What will you study?

    As your group starts a new study, this is a great time to take on a new role or change roles of service in your group. What new role will you take on? If you are uncertain, maybe your group members have some ideas for you. Remember you aren't making a lifetime commitment to the new role; it will be only for a few weeks. Also, consider sharing a role with another group member if you don't feel ready to serve solo.

SHARING   10 *min.*

To live worthy of God means to live in a way that is consistent with God's character, a way that is consistent with who we are because of faith in Christ.

15. What can you do to encourage believers in your sphere of influence to live lives worthy of God?

16. During the course of this four-week study, you have made commitments to share Jesus with the people in your life, either in

inviting your believing friends to grow in Christian community or by sharing the gospel in words or actions with unbelievers. Share with the group any highlights that you have experienced as you've stepped out in faith to share with others.

SURRENDERING   *10 min.*

Psalm 106:1 says: "Give thanks to the LORD, for he is good; his love endures forever." It is good to remember and give thanks for what the Lord has done.

17. Look back over the *Prayer and Praise Report.* Are there any answered prayers? Spend a few minutes sharing these in simple, one-sentence prayers of thanks to God. It's important to share your praises along with prayer requests so you can see where God is working in your lives.

18. Close by praying for your prayer requests. Also, take a couple of minutes to review the praises you have recorded on the *Prayer and Praise Report.* Thank God for what he's done in your group during this study.

For Deeper Study (Optional)

Read and reflect on Psalm 110, a royal psalm that foreshadows the coming of the Messiah. God's Anointed is declared to be king and priest forever.

Psalm 110 can be divided into the following three parts:

- The Lord's enthronement of David's Lord, vv. 1–3
- The king's Melchizedekian priesthood, v. 4
- The Lord's protection of his Anointed, vv. 5–7

For more on the significance of "the order of Melchizedek," read Hebrews 7.

Reflections

The Lord promised Joshua success and prosperity in Joshua 1:8 when he said, "Do not let this Book of the Law depart from your mouth; meditate on it day and night, so that you may be careful to do everything written in it. Then you will be prosperous and successful." We too can claim this promise for our lives as we commit to meditate on the Word of God each day. As in previous weeks, read and meditate on the daily verses and record any insights you gain in the space provided. Summarize what you have learned this week on Day 6.

Day 1. He will endure as long as the sun, as long as the moon, through all generations (Ps. 72:5).

REFLECT

_____

_____

_____

_____

Day 2. You said, "I have made a covenant with my chosen one, I have sworn to David my servant, 'I will establish your line forever and make your throne firm through all generations'" (Ps. 89:3–4).

REFLECT

_____

_____

_____

_____

Day 3. Now I know that the LORD saves his anointed; he answers him from his holy heaven with the saving power of his right hand (Ps. 20:6).

REFLECT

_____

_____

_____

_____

Day 4. O LORD, the king rejoices in your strength. How great is his joy in the victories you give! You have granted him the desire of his heart and have not withheld the request of his lips (Ps. 21:1–2).

REFLECT

_____

_____

_____

_____

Day 5. He is my loving God and my fortress, my stronghold and my deliverer, my shield, in whom I take refuge, who subdues peoples under me (Ps. 144:2).

REFLECT

_____

_____

_____

_____

Day 6. Use the following space to write any thoughts God has put in your heart and mind about the things we have looked at in this session and during your time this week.

SUMMARY

_____

_____

_____

_____

APPENDIX

FREQUENTLY ASKED QUESTIONS

What do we do on the first night of our group?
Like all fun things in life—have a party! A "get to know you" coffee, dinner, or dessert is a great way to launch a new study. You may want to review the *Small Group Agreement* and share the names of a few friends you can invite to join you. But most importantly, have fun before your study time begins.

Where do we find new members for our group?
This can be challenging, especially for new groups that have only a few people or for existing groups that lose a few people along the way. Pray with your group and then brainstorm a list of people from work, church, your neighborhood, your children's school, family, the gym, and so forth. Then have each group member invite several of the people on his or her list. Another strategy is to ask church leaders to announce that your group is open to new members.

No matter how you find members, it's vital that you stay on the lookout for new people to join your group. All groups tend to go through healthy attrition—the result of moves, releasing new leaders, ministry opportunities, and so forth—and if the group gets too small, it could be at risk of shutting down. If you and your group stay open, you'll be amazed at the people God sends your way. The next person just might become a friend for life. You never know!

How long will this group meet?
It's up to the group—once you come to the end of this study. Most groups meet weekly for at least their first six months, but every other week can work as well. We recommend that the group meet for the first six months on a weekly basis if possible. This allows for continuity, and if people miss a meeting, they aren't gone for a whole month.

At the end of this study, each group member may decide whether he or she wants to continue on for another study. Some groups launch relationships that last for years, and others are stepping-stones into another group experience. Either way, enjoy the journey.

What if this group is not working for me?

Personality conflicts, life stage differences, geographical distance, level of spiritual maturity, or any number of things can cause you to feel the group doesn't work for you. Relax. Pray for God's direction, and at the end of this study decide whether to continue with this group or find another. You don't buy the first car you look at or marry the first person you date, and the same goes with a group. Don't bail out before the study is finished—God might have something to teach you. Also, don't run from conflict or prejudge people before you have given them a chance. God is still working in you too!

Who is the leader?

Most groups have an official leader. But ideally, the group will mature and members will share the facilitation of meetings. Healthy groups share hosting and leading. This ensures that all members grow, give their unique contribution, and develop their gifts. This study guide and the Holy Spirit can keep things on track even when you share leadership. Christ has promised to be in your midst as you gather. Ultimately, God is your leader each step of the way.

How do we handle the child care needs in our group?

This can be a sensitive issue. We suggest that you empower the group to openly brainstorm solutions. Try one option that works for a while and then adjust over time. Our favorite approach is for adults to share the cost of a babysitter (or two) who can watch the kids in a different part of the house. In this way, parents don't have to be away from their young children all evening. A second option is to use one home for the kids and a second home (close by) for the adults. A third idea is to rotate the adults who provide a lesson or care for the children either in the same home or in another home nearby. This can be an incredible blessing for kids. Finally, the most common idea is to decide that you need to have a night to invest in your spiritual lives individually or as a couple, and make your own arrangements for child care. Whatever the decision, the best approach is to dialogue openly about both the problem and the solution.

SMALL GROUP CALENDAR

Planning and calendaring can help ensure the greatest participation at every meeting. At the end of each meeting, review this calendar. Be sure to include a regular rotation of host homes and leaders, and don't forget birthdays, socials, church events, holidays, and mission/ ministry projects.

Date	Lesson	Dessert/Meal	Role

SMALL GROUP AGREEMENT

Our Purpose

To transform our spiritual lives by cultivating our spiritual health in a healthy small group community. In addition, we:

_____

_____

_____

Our Values

Group Attendance	To give priority to the group meeting. We will call or e-mail if we will be late or absent. (Completing the *Small Group Calendar* will minimize this issue.)
Safe Environment	To help create a safe place where people can be heard and feel loved. (Please, no quick answers, snap judgments, or simple fixes.)
Respect Differences	To be gentle and gracious to people with different spiritual maturity, personal opinions, temperaments, or imperfections. We are all works in progress.
Confidentiality	To keep anything that is shared strictly confidential and within the group, and avoid sharing improper information about those outside the group.
Encouragement for Growth	To be not just takers but givers of life. We want to spiritually multiply our lives by serving others with our God-given gifts.
Welcome for Newcomers	To keep an open chair and share Jesus's dream of finding a shepherd for every sheep.
Shared Ownership	To remember that every member is a minister and to ensure that each attender will share a small team role or responsibility over time. (See the *Team Roles*.)
Rotating Hosts/ Leaders and Homes	To encourage different people to host the group in their homes, and to rotate the responsibility of facilitating each meeting. (See the *Small Group Calendar*.)

Our Expectations

- Refreshments/mealtimes _____

- Child care _____

- When we will meet (day of week) _____

- Where we will meet (place) _____

- We will begin at (time) _____ and end at _____

- We will do our best to have some or all of us attend a worship service together. Our primary worship service time will be _____

- Date of this agreement _____

- Date we will review this agreement again _____

- Who (other than the leader) will review this agreement at the end of this study _____

TEAM ROLES

The Bible makes clear that every member, not just the small group leader, is a minister in the body of Christ. In a healthy small group, every member takes on some small role or responsibility. It can be more fun and effective if you team up on these roles.

Review the team roles and responsibilities below, and have each member volunteer for a role or participate on a team. If someone doesn't know where to serve or is holding back, as a group, suggest a team or role. It's best to have one or two people on each team so you have each of the five purposes covered. Serving in even a small capacity will not only help your leader but also will make the group more fun for everyone. Don't hold back. Join a team!

The opportunities below are broken down by the five purposes and then by a *crawl* (beginning), *walk* (intermediate), or *run* (advanced) role. Try to cover at least the crawl and walk roles, and select a role that matches your group, your gifts, and your maturity.

Team Roles	Team Player(s)
CONNECTING TEAM (Fellowship and Community Building)	
Crawl: Host a social event or group activity in the first week or two.	
Walk: Create a list of uncommitted friends and then invite them to an open house or group social.	
Run: Plan a twenty-four-hour retreat or weekend getaway for the group. Lead the *Connecting* time each week for the group.	
GROWING TEAM (Discipleship and Spiritual Growth)	
Crawl: Coordinate the spiritual partners for the group. Facilitate a three- or four-person discussion circle during the Bible study portion of your meeting. Coordinate the discussion circles.	

58

Team Roles	Team Player(s)
Walk: Tabulate the *Personal Health Plans* in a summary to let people know how you're doing as a group.	
Encourage personal devotions through group discussions and pairing up with spiritual (accountability) partners.	
Run: Take the group on a prayer walk, or plan a day of solitude, fasting, or personal retreat.	

SERVING TEAM (Discovering Your God-Given Design for Ministry)

Crawl: Ensure that every member finds a group role or team he or she enjoys.	
Walk: Have every member take a gift test and determine your group's gifts.	
Plan a ministry project together.	
Run: Help each member decide on a way to use his or her unique gifts somewhere in the church.	

SHARING TEAM (Sharing and Evangelism)

Crawl: Coordinate the group's *Prayer and Praise Report* of friends and family who don't know Christ.	
Walk: Search for group mission opportunities and plan a cross-cultural group activity.	
Run: Take a small group "vacation" to host a six-week group in your neighborhood or office. Then come back together with your current group.	

SURRENDERING TEAM (Surrendering Your Heart to Worship)

Crawl: Maintain the group's *Pray and Praise Report* or journal.	
Walk: Lead a brief time of worship each week (at the beginning or end of your meeting), either a cappella or using a song from the DVD or a worship CD.	
Run: Plan a unique time of worship through Communion, foot washing, night of prayer, or nature walking.	

PERSONAL HEALTH PLAN

This worksheet could become your single most important feature in this study. On it you can record your personal priorities before the Father. It will help you live a healthy spiritual life, balancing all five of God's purposes.

You will develop your *Personal Health Plan* as you move through the study material in this study guide. At appropriate places during the study, you will be instructed to identify your progress in one or more of the purpose areas (connect, grow, develop, share, surrender) by answering the question associated with the purpose. You may be instructed to discuss with your spiritual partner your progress on one or more steps, and record your progress and the progress of your spiritual partner on the *Progress Report*.

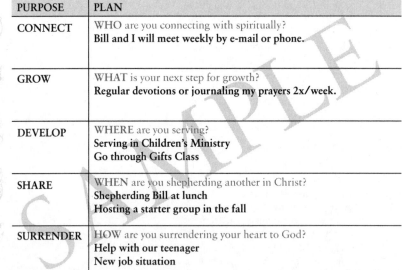

	PURPOSE	PLAN
	CONNECT	WHO are you connecting with spiritually? **Bill and I will meet weekly by e-mail or phone.**
	GROW	WHAT is your next step for growth? **Regular devotions or journaling my prayers 2x/week.**
	DEVELOP	WHERE are you serving? **Serving in Children's Ministry** **Go through Gifts Class**
	SHARE	WHEN are you shepherding another in Christ? **Shepherding Bill at lunch** **Hosting a starter group in the fall**
	SURRENDER	HOW are you surrendering your heart to God? **Help with our teenager** **New job situation**

PURPOSE	PLANNING QUESTION
CONNECT	WHO are you connecting with spiritually?
GROW	WHAT is your next step for growth?
DEVELOP	WHERE are you serving?
SHARE	WHEN are you shepherding another in Christ?
SURRENDER	HOW are you surrendering your heart to God?

DATE	MY PROGRESS	PARTNER'S PROGRESS
3/5	Talked during our group	Figured out our goals together
3/12	Missed our time together	Missed our time together
3/26	Met for coffee and review of my goals	Met for coffee
4/10	E-mailed prayer requests	Praying for partner and group
5/5	Great start on personal journaling	Read Mark 1–6 in one sitting!
5/12	Traveled and not doing well this week	Journaled about Christ as healer
5/26	Back on track	Busy and distracted; asked for prayer
6/1	Need to call Children's Pastor	Scared to lead worship
6/26	Group did a serving project together	Agreed to lead group worship
6/30	Regularly rotating leadership	Led group worship–great job!
7/5	Called Jim to see if he's open to joining our group	Wanted to invite somebody, but didn't
7/12	Preparing to start a group in fall	
7/30	Group prayed for me	Told friend something I'm learning about Christ
8/5	Overwhelmed but encouraged	Absent from group today
8/15	Felt heard and more settled	Issue with wife
8/30	Read book on teens	Glad he took on his fear
9/5	Talked during our group	Figured out our goals together
9/12	Missed our time together	Missed our time together

Progress Report

DATE	MY PROGRESS	PARTNER'S PROGRESS

SERVING COMMUNION

Churches vary in their treatment of *Communion* (or *The Lord's Supper*). We offer one simple form by which a small group can share this experience together. You can adapt this as necessary, or omit it from your group altogether, depending on your church's beliefs.

Steps in Serving Communion

1. Open by sharing about God's love, forgiveness, grace, mercy, commitment, tenderheartedness, faithfulness, etc., out of your personal journey (connect with the stories of those in the room).
2. Read the passage: "And he took bread, gave thanks and broke it, and gave it to them, saying, 'This is my body given for you; do this in remembrance of me'" (Luke 22:19).
3. Pray and pass the bread around the circle.
4. When everyone has been served, remind them that this represents Jesus's broken body on their behalf. Simply state, "Jesus said, 'Do this in remembrance of me' (Luke 22:19). Let us eat together," and eat the bread as a group.
5. Then read the rest of the passage: "In the same way, after the supper he took the cup, saying, 'This cup is the new covenant in my blood, which is poured out for you'" (Luke 22:20).
6. Pray and serve the cups, either by passing a small tray, serving them individually, or having members pick up a cup from the table.
7. When everyone has been served, remind them the juice represents Christ's blood shed for them, then simply state, "Take and drink in remembrance of him. Let us drink together."
8. Finish by singing a simple song, listening to a praise song, or having a time of prayer in thanks to God.

Communion passages: Matthew 26:26–29; Mark 14:22–25; Luke 22:14–20; 1 Corinthians 10:16–21; 11:17–34

PERFORMING A FOOTWASHING

Scripture: John 13:1–17. Jesus makes it quite clear to his disciples that his position as the Father's Son includes being a servant rather than being one of power and glory only.

The Purpose of Footwashing

To properly understand the scene and the intention of Jesus, we must realize that the washing of feet was the duty of slaves and indeed of non-Jewish rather than Jewish slaves. Jesus placed himself in the position of a servant. He displayed to the disciples self-sacrifice and love. In view of his majesty, only the symbolic position of a slave was adequate to open their eyes and keep them from lofty illusions. The point of footwashing, then, is to correct the attitude that Jesus discerned in the disciples. It constitutes the permanent basis for mutual service, service in your group and for the community around you, which is laid on all Christians.

When to Implement

There are three primary places we would recommend you insert a footwashing:

- during a break in the *Surrendering* section of your group
- during a break in the *Growing* section of your group
- at the closing of your group

A special time of prayer for each person as he or she gets his or her feet washed can be added to the footwashing time.

SURRENDERING AT THE CROSS

Surrendering everything to God is one of the most challenging aspects of following Jesus. It involves a relationship built on trust and faith. Each of us is in a different place on our spiritual journey. Some of us have known the Lord for many years, some are new in our faith, and some may still be checking God out. Regardless, we all have things that we still want control over—things we don't want to give to God because we don't know what he will do with them. These things are truly more important to us than God is—they have become our god.

We need to understand that God wants us to be completely devoted to him. If we truly love God with all our heart, soul, strength, and mind (Luke 10:27), we will be willing to give him everything.

Steps in Surrendering at the Cross

1. You will need some small pieces of paper and pens or pencils for people to write down the things they want to sacrifice/surrender to God.
2. If you have a wooden cross, hammers, and nails, you can have the members nail their sacrifices to the cross. If you don't have a wooden cross, get creative. Think of another way to symbolically relinquish the sacrifices to God. You might use a fireplace to burn them in the fire as an offering to the Lord. The point is giving to the Lord whatever hinders your relationship with him.
3. Create an atmosphere conducive to quiet reflection and prayer. Whatever this quiet atmosphere looks like for your group, do the best you can to create a peaceful time to meet with God.
4. Once you are settled, prayerfully think about the points below. Let the words and thoughts draw you into a heart-to-heart connection with your Lord Jesus Christ.

   ☐ **Worship him.** Ask God to change your viewpoint so you can worship him through a surrendered spirit.

☐ **Humble yourself.** Surrender doesn't happen without humility. James 4:6–7 says, "'God opposes the proud but gives grace to the humble.' Submit yourselves, then, to God."

☐ **Surrender your mind, will, and emotions.** This is often the toughest part of surrendering. What do you sense God urging you to give him so you can have the kind of intimacy he desires with you? Our hearts yearn for this kind of connection with him; let go of the things that stand between you.

☐ **Write out your prayer.** Write out your prayer of sacrifice and surrender to the Lord. This may be an attitude, a fear, a person, a job, a possession—anything that God reveals is a hindrance to your relationship with him.

5. After writing out your sacrifice, take it to the cross and offer it to the Lord. Nail your sacrifice to the cross, or burn it as a sacrifice in the fire.

6. Close by singing, praying together, or taking communion. Make this time as short or as long as seems appropriate for your group.

Surrendering to God is life-changing and liberating. God desires that we be overcomers! First John 4:4 says, "You, dear children, are from God and have overcome . . . because the one who is in you is greater than the one who is in the world."

PRAYER AND PRAISE REPORT

Briefly share your prayer requests with the large group, making notations below. Then gather in small groups of two to four to pray for each other.

SESSION 1

Prayer Requests

_____

_____

_____

_____

Praise Reports

_____

_____

_____

_____

SESSION 2

Prayer Requests

_____
_____
_____
_____
_____

Praise Reports

_____
_____
_____
_____
_____

SESSION 3

Prayer Requests

_____
_____
_____
_____
_____

Praise Reports

_____
_____
_____
_____
_____

SESSION 4

Prayer Requests

_____

_____

_____

_____

_____

Praise Reports

_____

_____

_____

_____

_____

LEADING FOR THE FIRST TIME
LEADERSHIP 101

Sweaty palms are a healthy sign. The Bible says God is gracious to the humble. Remember who is in control; the time to worry is when you're *not* worried. Those who are soft in heart (and sweaty palmed) are those whom God is sure to speak through.

Seek support. Ask your leader, co-leader, or close friend to pray for you and prepare with you before the session. Walking through the study will help you anticipate potentially difficult questions and discussion topics.

Bring your uniqueness to the study. Lean into who you are and how God wants you to uniquely lead the study.

Prepare. Prepare. Prepare. Go through the session several times. If you are using the DVD, listen to the teaching segment and *Leader Lifter*. Consider writing in a journal or fasting for a day to prepare yourself for what God wants to do.

Don't wait until the last minute to prepare.

Ask for feedback so you can grow. Perhaps in an e-mail or on cards handed out at the study, have everyone write down three things you did well and one thing you could improve on. Don't get defensive, but show an openness to learn and grow.

Prayerfully consider launching a new group. This doesn't need to happen overnight, but God's heart is for this to happen over time. Not all Christians are called to be leaders or teachers, but we are all called to be "shepherds" of a few someday.

Share with your group what God is doing in your heart. God is searching for those whose hearts are fully his. Share your trials and victories. We promise that people will relate.

Prayerfully consider whom you would like to pass the baton to next week. It's only fair. God is ready for the next member of your group to go on the faith journey you just traveled. Make it fun, and expect God to do the rest.

LEADER'S NOTES
INTRODUCTION

Congratulations! You have responded to the call to help shepherd Jesus's flock. There are few other tasks in the family of God that surpass the contribution you will be making. We have provided you several ways to prepare for this role. Between the *Read Me First*, these *Leader's Notes*, and the *Watch This First* and *Leader Lifter* segments on the optional *Deepening Life Together: Psalms* Video Teaching DVD, you'll have all you need to do a great job of leading your group. Just don't forget, you are not alone. God knew that you would be asked to lead this group and he won't let you down. In Hebrews 13:5b God promises us, "Never will I leave you; never will I forsake you."

Your role as leader is to create a safe, warm environment for your group. As a leader, your most important job is to create an atmosphere where people are willing to talk honestly about what the topics discussed in this study have to do with them. Be available before people arrive so you can greet them at the door. People are naturally nervous at a new group, so a hug or handshake can help put them at ease. Before you start leading your group, a little preparation will give you confidence. Review the *Read Me First* at the front of your study guide so you'll understand the purpose of each section, enabling you to help your group understand it as well.

If you're new to leading a group, congratulations and thank you; this will be a life-changing experience for you also. We have provided these *Leader's Notes* to help new leaders begin well.

It's important in your first meeting to make sure group members understand that things shared personally and in prayer must remain confidential. Also, be careful not to dominate the group discussion, but facilitate it and encourage others to join in and share. And lastly, have fun.

Take a moment at the beginning of your first meeting to orient the group to one principle that undergirds this study: A healthy small group balances the purposes of the church. Most small groups emphasize Bible study, fellowship, and prayer. But God has called us to reach out to others as well. He wants us to do what Jesus teaches, not just learn about it.

Preparing for each meeting ahead of time. Take the time to review the session, the *Leader's Notes*, and the optional *Leader Lifter* for the session before each session. Also write down your answers to each question. Pay special attention to exercises that ask group members to *do* something. These exercises will help your group live out what the Bible teaches, not just talk about it. Be sure you understand how the exercises work, and bring any supplies you might need, such as paper or pens. Pray for your group members by name at least once between sessions and before each session. Use the *Prayer and Praise Report* so you will remember their prayer requests. Ask God to use your time together to touch the heart of every person. Expect God to give you the opportunity to talk with those he wants you to encourage or challenge in a special way.

Don't try to go it alone. Pray for God to help you. Ask other members of your group to help by taking on some small role. In the *Appendix* you'll find the *Team Roles* pages with some suggestions to get people involved. Leading is more rewarding if you give group members opportunities to help. Besides, helping group members discover their individual gifts for serving or even leading the group will bless all of you.

Consider asking a few people to come early to help set up, pray, and introduce newcomers to others. Even if everyone is new, they don't know that yet and may be shy when they arrive. You might give people roles like setting up name tags or handing out drinks. This could be a great way to spot a co-leader.

Subgrouping. If your group has more than seven people, break into discussion groups of three to four people for the *Growing* and *Surrendering* sections each week. People will connect more with the study and each other when they have more opportunity to participate. Smaller discussion circles encourage quieter people to talk more and tend to minimize the effects of more vocal or dominant members. Also, people who are unaccustomed to praying aloud will feel more comfortable praying within a smaller group of people. Share prayer requests in the larger group and then break into smaller groups to pray for each other. People are more willing to pray in small circles if they know that the whole group will hear all the prayer requests.

Memorizing Scripture. At the start of each session you will find a memory verse—a verse for the group to memorize each week. Encourage your group members to do this. Memorizing God's Word is both directed and celebrated throughout the Bible, either explicitly ("Your word I have hidden in my heart, that I might not sin against You" [Ps. 119:11 NKJV]), or implicitly, as in the example of our Lord ("He departed to the mountain to pray" [Mark 6:46 NKJV]).

Anyone who has memorized Scripture can confirm the amazing spiritual benefits that result from this practice. Don't miss out on the opportunity to encourage your group to grow in the knowledge of God's Word through Scripture memorization.

Reflections. We've provided opportunity for a personal time with God using the *Reflections* at the end of each session. Don't press seekers to do this, but just remind the group that every believer should have a plan for personal time with God.

Inviting new people. Cast the vision, as Jesus did, to be inclusive, not exclusive. Ask everyone to prayerfully think of people who would enjoy or benefit from a group like this—then invite them. The beginning of a new study is a great time to welcome a few people into your circle. Don't worry about ending up with too many people—you can always have one discussion circle in the living room and another in the dining room.

For Deeper Study (Optional). We have included a *For Deeper Study* section in most sessions. *For Deeper Study* provides additional passages for individual study on the topic of each session. If your group likes to do deeper Bible study, consider having members study the *For Deeper Study* passages for homework. Then, during the *Growing* portion of your meeting, you can share the high points of what you've learned.

LEADER'S NOTES

SESSIONS

Session One Psalms of Praise

Connecting

1. We've designed this study for both new and established groups, and for both seekers and the spiritually mature. New groups will need to invest more time building relationships with each other. Established groups often want to dig deeper into Bible study and application. Regardless of whether your group is new or has been together for a while, be sure to take time to connect at this first session.

2. Most of us have celebrated our loved ones' birthdays, anniversaries, promotions, etc., by singing or speaking words of adoration and respect.

3. A very important item in this first session is the *Small Group Agreement*. An agreement helps clarify your group's priorities and cast new vision for what the group can become. You can find this in the *Appendix* of this study guide. We've found that groups that talk about these values up front and commit to an agreement benefit significantly. They work through conflicts long before people get to the point of frustration, so there's a lot less pain.

   Take some time to review this agreement before your meeting. Then during your meeting, read the agreement aloud to the entire group. If some people have concerns about a specific item or the agreement as a whole, be sensitive to their concerns. Explain that tens of thousands of groups use agreements like this one as a simple tool for building trust and group health over time.

Growing

Have someone read Bible passages aloud. It's a good idea to ask ahead of time, because not everyone is comfortable reading aloud in public.

4. The psalmist describes God with words like "majestic" (v. 1) and names things God has done, like creating the stars and galaxies. He uses poetic images, imagining God as a craftsman using "fingers" (v. 3) to shape the heavens, even though he's well aware that God the Father doesn't have literal fingers.

5. God set his glory above the heavens. Nothing beneath them can praise him adequately. There is always a sense of wonder and awe at what God has placed outside or beyond our realm.

6. When wondering at the magnificence of creation, we cannot help but be reminded how small we are in the midst of such greatness. This realization of our own smallness brings us to a place of awe at the greatness of the Creator. We desperately need to cultivate awe before God, because awe helps us see things in perspective. It protects us from pride and from the foolish things we believe and do because of pride.

7. The works of God's hands include *everything* he created. That could mean that all of planet Earth is our playground to exploit as we like. But is that the way God expects authorities to behave? More likely, planet Earth is our responsibility to care for.

8. We must remove ourselves from the busyness of life to focus on and contemplate God's creation: walk on the beach and consider the vastness of the ocean, go on a hike in the mountains, take a nature walk, look at the sky on a cloudless night.

9. The two types of help identified in this psalm are a refuge or fortress where we can run to find shelter from the storm and inner strength with which we can endure our calamity.

10. We are the favored people of God over whom God pours his blessings today. We take refuge in him.

11. He will conquer enemy nations and restore peace and security to the nation of Israel. He will receive honor and glory.

Developing

This section enables you to help the group see the importance of developing their abilities for service to God.

14. Questions 14, 15: Spiritual partners will pair up during group time and/ or through the week and use the *Personal Health Plan* to record plans and progress throughout our study of Psalms. For many, spiritual partners will be a new idea, but we highly encourage you to try them for this study. It's hard to start a spiritual practice like prayer or consistent Bible reading with no support. A friend makes a huge difference.

We recommend that men partner with men and women partner with women. Partners can check in with each other weekly either during your group meetings or outside the meeting. As leader, you may want to prayerfully decide who would be a good match with whom. Try to discern who might have good relational chemistry that may lead to a deeper connection.

Remind people that this partnership isn't forever; it's just for a few weeks. Be sure to have extra copies of the *Personal Health Plan* available at this first meeting in case you need to have a group of three spiritual partners. It is a good idea for you to look over the *Personal Health Plan* before the meeting so you can help people understand how to use it.

Sharing

Jesus wants all of his disciples to help outsiders connect with him, to know him personally. This section should provide an opportunity to go beyond Bible study to biblical living.

16. We provided a *Circles of Life* diagram for you and the group to use to help you identify people who need to be connected in Christian community. When people are asked why they never go to church, they often say, "No one ever invited me." Remind the group that our responsibility is to invite people, but we are not responsible for how they respond. Talk to the group about the importance of inviting people; remind them that healthy small groups make a habit of inviting friends, neighbors, unconnected church members, co-workers, etc., to join their groups or join them at a weekend service. When people get connected to a group of new friends, they often join the church.

    The *Circles of Life* represent one of the values of the *Small Group Agreement*: "Welcome for Newcomers." Some groups fear that newcomers will interrupt the intimacy that members have built over time. However, groups generally gain strength with the infusion of new blood. It's like a river of living water flowing into a stagnant pond. Some groups remain permanently open, while others open periodically, such as at the beginning and ending of a study. Love grows by giving itself away. If your circle becomes too large for easy face-to-face conversations, you can simply form a second discussion circle in another room in your home.

Surrendering

God is most pleased by a heart that is fully his. Each session will provide group members a chance to surrender their hearts to God in prayer and worship. Group prayer requests and prayer time should be included every week.

18. This question is meant to encourage quiet time at home each day throughout the week. Here you can help the group see the importance of making time with God a priority. Read through this section and be prepared to help the group understand how important it is to fill our minds with the Word of God. If people already have a good Bible reading plan and commitment, that is great, but you may have people who struggle to stay in the Word daily.

Sometimes beginning with a simple commitment to a short daily reading can start a habit that changes a person's life. The *Reflections* pages at the end of each session include verses that were either talked about in the session or support the teaching of the session. They are very short readings with a few lines to encourage people to write down their thoughts. Remind the group about these *Reflections* each week after the *Surrendering* section. Encourage the group to commit to a next step in prayer, Bible reading, or meditation on the Word.

19. As you move to a time of sharing prayer requests, be sure to remind the group of the importance of confidentiality and keeping what is shared in the group within the group. Everyone must feel that the personal things they share will be kept in confidence if you are to have safety and bonding among group members.

    Use the *Prayer and Praise Report* in the *Appendix* to record your prayer requests. There you can keep track of requests and celebrate answers to prayer.

For Deeper Study

We have included an optional *For Deeper Study* section in most sessions. *For Deeper Study* provides additional passages for individual study on the topic of each session. If your group likes to do deeper Bible study, consider having members study the *For Deeper Study* passages at home between meetings.

Session Two Psalms of Lament

Growing

3. Psalm 3 is a prayer to God for help in the face of an enemy.

4. God does not fail to answer prayer. The psalmist is confident that God will protect him from harm and even from humiliation—which many of us fear more than physical harm.

5. While many lie awake at night consumed by the worries of the day, the psalmist remains confident in God to be his shield and deliverer, so he sleeps in peace. That sounds easy, but it isn't. Encourage the group to talk about how they have grown in this confidence over time, or how they struggle with it. We build this confidence by turning to God and his people when we suffer and experiencing how God cares for us.

6. The psalmist asks to be shielded or protected during his battle and ultimately for deliverance from, or victory over, his enemies.

7. Reflection can help us to find God at work in our lives when we might not otherwise notice.

9. God won't fall off his throne if we tell him the truth about the anger, fear, frustration, and confusion inside us. The psalms are his way of telling us that he welcomes honesty and doesn't want us to pretend to be joyful when we're not. He wants to be in the painful situation with us, helping us wrestle through it. He won't be threatened or vengeful the way some people are when we tell them what we really think. He knows that we sometimes need to go through these doubts and negative feelings in order to build secure confidence in him.

10. Ceaseless, day-and-night prayer only comes forth from a soul who holds onto the trust that God will hear and answer.

11. God is sovereign, and whether he causes suffering directly or allows it indirectly, he is working in, behind, and through it. When we don't understand the cause or reason behind our suffering, there is nothing to do except turn to God. The psalmist knows this. He acknowledges God's sovereignty in his suffering and his own inability to figure out why God is allowing it. He pleads his case to the God who saves.

12. It reminds us that life is full of troubles that can bring us to a point of despair if we forget God's faithfulness to work in the midst of them. It is in these most desperate of times when we most need to pause and remember what God has done and what God has promised to do for those who love him. These are the times for persistent, honest prayer, and God won't be upset if we can't immediately get to the other side of despair and say something hopeful.

Sharing

13. We too can share the good news of who Jesus is and what he has done wherever we go. If we believe the apostles' eyewitness accounts in the New Testament, and if we have a personal experience of Christ and the Holy Spirit, then we have a responsibility to tell others what we know.

Developing

16. Here is an opportunity for group members to consider where they can take a next step toward getting involved in ministering to the body of Christ in your local church. Encourage group members to use the *Personal Health Plan* to jot down their next step and plan how and when they will begin.

Session Three Psalms of Thanksgiving

Connecting

2. It's time to start thinking about what your group will do when you're finished with this study. Now is the time to ask how many people will be joining you so you can choose a study and have the books available when you meet for the next session.

Growing

4. The psalmist thanks God for giving him the strength to endure the battle, for being unshakably solid in an unstable situation, for being his place of rest/refuge, and for being his source of protection from harm. One of the central temptations in life is to look to sources other than God for strength. We may look to money or career, to our own inner resources, to military equipment, or to other people. While all of these have their place, they will let us down if we place them in the position God should have.

6. God rewarded David for his devoted heart and life of service. This is not a proud boast of perfection but an honest declaration of God's willingness to reward those who love him. No one does right all the time, but generally speaking, God blesses those who try to live for him. Those who go their own way are left to bring misery upon themselves.

7. We may be tempted to say no. And a good biblical example of a time when this explanation appears untrue is Job. Even though he lived his life righteously before God, he was allowed to suffer. Also, there may be times when the wicked prosper. But in the long run, the righteous will be blessed and the unrighteous will be judged. As Christ's followers, we must remember that even when this doesn't seem true in this life on earth, it will be true at the final judgment that everyone faces beyond this life. Those who live in relationship with God will be blessed. Those who turn away will be judged.

8. The first telling focuses on God as the deliverer. The second telling focuses on David as the delivered. David wasn't passive—he fought. But he knew God was his source of skill and strength. David and God were partners, and David gives God credit for making the victory possible.

11. Phrases such as "lifted me out of the depths," "brought me up from the grave," and "spared me from . . . the pit" lead us to believe that the psalmist was so ill he possibly was near death.

    This sets the tone for the great contrast that is found throughout this psalm. The greater the deliverance, the greater the praise or thankfulness.

12. There is imminent death—eminent life; illness—health; God's anger—God's favor; weeping—rejoicing; sin—repentance; grief—joy. This all adds up to

the contrast between disorientation and reorientation, and this is the shift the psalmist is most thankful for.

13. God's anger is temporary (v. 5). He is gracious simply because it is in his character to be gracious. He is merciful, so we can ask him for mercy (v. 8).

Sharing

18. It is important to return to the *Circles of Life* and engage the group in identifying people who need to know Christ more deeply. Encourage a commitment to praying for God's guidance and an opportunity to share with each person named in the *Circles*.

Session Four Royal Psalms

Growing

3. According to verse 2, the nations are conspiring against God's "Anointed One." This refers first to the human king at that time, because it was the custom for the Israelites to anoint a man with oil when he became king. In this sense, every king was an anointed one. However, the ultimate Anointed One is the Messiah. It is futile to rebel against what God has ordained.

4. God mocks the rebellious leaders in a scoffing laugh. It is ridiculous for anyone to think they can usurp God's plan. This is the only place in Scripture where God is said to laugh. He rebukes them and terrifies them with his wrath and promises to install his King on Zion.

5. The kingdom of the Anointed One will extend to the "ends of the earth." We can imagine people thinking of the king of that time as God's adopted son, and we can imagine the poet speaking of the king's triumph over enemy nations in broad terms. But ultimately the psalmist knew that this king was never going to rule over all things. That could only be true of the Messiah, whose kingdom would embrace all of creation and not just the Jews but all the nations of the earth.

6. The Lord warns them to be wise, and to serve the Lord with fear and trembling.

7. All who take refuge in the Son will be blessed. That's an extreme thing to say about a human king, but reasonable to say about the divine Son of God. A human king might have wrath that enemies should be wary of, but this verse makes claims about a king who is like the claims the psalmists make elsewhere about God.

8. The psalmist praises the king for his gracious and anointed speech; his military victories for the sake of truth, humility, and righteousness; his pursuit of justice and righteousness.

9. The king was supposed to reflect God's character and not merely be the kind of self-serving tyrant who ruled the pagan nations. Unfortunately, Judah's kings often fell far short of this standard. Jesus, however, fully embodies this vision of true kingship. His victories in this world—and consequently the victories of the Christian—are not military conquests but triumphs over the world system of values. We need to keep that focus in mind and not be distracted by the allure of power and military might.

11. The bride is advised to forget her past, focus intently on her future with the king, and look ahead to what the future will bring.

12. The church is the bride of Christ. And just as the royal bride is asked to forget her past in order to serve her groom with loyalty and honor, we are to be careful not to allow any human relationship to hinder us from wholeheartedly pursuing and serving God. As we do this, we will receive blessings as the bride of Christ, including the love of the King as well as joy and gladness that come from being in his presence.

Sharing

15. One of the best things you can do is to set an example—if you do, then others will do what you are doing.

16. Allow one or two group members to share for a few minutes a testimony about how they helped someone connect in Christian community or shared Jesus with an unbelieving friend or relative.

Surrendering

17. Spend a few minutes devoted solely to sharing praises aloud in simple, one-sentence prayers. Be sure to allow time to share prayer requests. Have one person close the meeting with prayer.

SMALL GROUP ROSTER

Name	Address	Phone	E-mail Address	Team or Role	When/How to Contact You

Pass your book around your group at your first meeting to get every-one's name and contact information.

Name	Address	Phone	E-mail Address	Team or Role	When/How to Contact You

DEEPENING LIFE TOGETHER SERIES

Six **NEW** Studies Now Available!

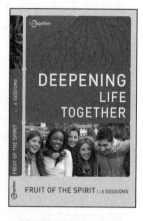

FRUIT OF THE SPIRIT

JAMES

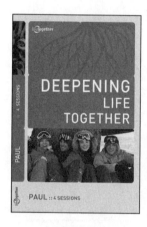

PAUL

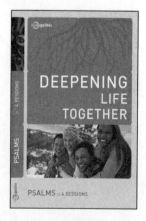

PSALMS

RUTH

SERMON ON THE MOUNT

Deepening Life Together is an innovative approach to group Bible study in a DVD format built on the five biblical purposes: **connecting, growing, developing, sharing, and surrendering.**

Each session includes a traditional study guide and a DVD with insightful teaching from trusted scholars and pastors. Included on each DVD are pre-session training videos for leaders and footage from the bestselling *Jesus Film*.

Lifetogether has developed and sold over 2.5 million copies of bestselling, award-winning curriculum for small groups. This DVD series—perfect for small group ministries, Sunday school classes, and Bible study groups—will improve your worship, fellowship, discipleship, evangelism, and ministry.

Studies Available:

ACTS

PRAYING GOD'S WAY

EPHESIANS

PROMISES OF GOD

JOHN

PARABLES

REVELATION

ROMANS

DEEPENING LIFE TOGETHER KIT

The kit includes 8 discussion guides and 8 DVDs: Acts, Romans, John, Ephesians, Revelation, Praying God's Way, Promises of God, and Parables

BakerBooks
a division of Baker Publishing Group
www.BakerBooks.com